www.finishinglinepress.com

Heliotropic

poems by

Doug Bootes

Finishing Line Press
Georgetown, Kentucky

Heliotropic

Copyright © 2024 by Doug Bootes
ISBN 979-8-88838-535-7 First Edition
All rights reserved under International and Pan-American Copyright Conventions.
No part of this book may be reproduced in any manner whatsoever without written
permission from the publisher, except in the case of brief quotations embodied in
critical articles and reviews.

ACKNOWLEDGMENTS

Thank you to the following:

Watercolor Fridge Magnet is published as Refrigerator Watercolor
Ekphrastic in *The Closed Eye Open: Maya's Micros Feature*
Hummingbird Outslick appeared in *Poetry Northwest*
Southpaw was published by *Runestone Journal*
Invasive Species was published in *Voice the Spiriture: Neo Modern Literature
from the Institute of American Indian Arts*
We are Each Other's Harvest was included under the title The Web in
Accolades: Santa Fe Community College Writing Awards

Publisher: Leah Huete de Maines
Editor: Christen Kincaid
Cover Art: Doug Bootes
Author Photo: Doug Bootes
Cover Design: Elizabeth Maines McCleavy

Order online: www.finishinglinepress.com
also available on amazon.com

Author inquiries and mail orders:
Finishing Line Press
PO Box 1626
Georgetown, Kentucky 40324
USA

Contents

The natural search for light can be referred to as the "heliotropic effect," which simply means that every living system has a tendency toward light and away from darkness, or a tendency towards that which is life-giving and away from that which endangers life.

Hummingbird Outslick

Misnomer living
    make-shift
        abandon,
Father,
    Protector,
        Spirit,
    Inmate,
    Been a lot of things
        From here to Apalachicola,
Another name corrupted,
    mis placed,
    dis placed,
        Damned to eternal erasure.
        Never know what you'll find
            up my skirt—
                annotated chromosomes,
                    chinquapin hogsuckers,
                        OxyContin Pentecost,
                blinding corn liquor headlights.
        So, curl on down
            into pot sherds and sand,
Blue gramma and rhyolite,
    crawl under the buffalo.
        Badger and coyote
            hunt together tonight.

Milkweed

Waiting out blossom explosions,
I would pry open pods

Pellet seeds peaceful
In their coma times five.

Milky membrane rows
And six decades later,

Reassemble latex glyphs
Onto rice paper plain,

Liberated pictographs roam
Grainy reflections of blue.

I've always been drawn
By the blown apart shattered

The way gray lead shotguns
A crisp November sky

Pinball through fibers
Come to rest   where exotic

  unexpected   unfamiliar

Under a struggling lung
Or sleeping beneath bridges

A last breath's echo or
Snarled traffic up ahead

A vacant lot unmoved
Or smoke twisting clouds.

Summer flowers may never comprehend
Angiosperm arithmetic,

Can't leave their posts
To count children off safely

May never know who sprouted
Or who suffers winter soil

Who's swallowed then expelled
Lying spent   after the fall.

Asclepius only knows
Ever reach upward,

Rise above what's given
In rooted soil below

Sun crying raindrops
Not theirs to decide

Who may or may not nurture—
As a monarch larva spreads

Unlikely honeyed wings,
So crisp paisley wombs

Birth ten thousand antelope horns
Into tomorrow's spring grassland.

Barrier Island Gulf Stream

Basking in the sun, our discordant coastlines migrate. Morpho
  dynamic sands become aeolian
dunes, their height proportionate to the weight of cavitation in a
  December hurricane. We're
bioturbation offspring stepping a slow-motion tango. Are you a
  mosquito magnet? Do your
pheromones have what it takes? There's more to the view than meets
  the sea, my friend.
Fossilized shark teeth wash ashore during the second year of April.
  Collect and keep them in a
sky-blue glass for optimal freshness. Despite sharply worn edges,
  many recall chartreuse
phosphorescence. If placed in gums, show some restraint nipping
  your lover's eye tonight.

Only four humans stay year-round—if you're one, beware the
  acrobatic antics of
strangler figs. Ghost orchid tribe slips past the guards around dawn,
  setting palm fronds free—
streaming peacock paradise atop shell mounds testified upward. What
  you will find in mangrove
tunnels and caves is the womb of a universe; biospheres of diversity in
  the water, on the land and
in the air, refuge for beautifully dangerous remnants of the last world.
  At the end of the day,
when the alluvial consort of the stone house and the green flash
  conflate a perfect union, sun skin
vibrates, searing wave-like ripples across the horizon, blasting super
  high clouds up against
burnished ether.

       O, how they keep climbing and climbing—

Watercolor Fridge Magnet
for John Prine

Over a crudely drawn landscape
gods loom in distress
made in our image—
the missing years;
reach stick figure hands
for thanksgiving clouds
      or charlotte's dewy web
pals 'til the massacre begins

Great rain, refrain.

Cornflakes cuss
loud as burnt bacon,
spilt milk prayers
cryin' on the tile,
stains in the sink
refusin' to erase,
watch rivers run dry
washin' tears for themselves

Great rain, great rain.

Watch headlights brush
Picassos on the wall
tired floor creaks
alcohol
      crickets
sittin' on the porch
          out front
I brought the cups tonight
you bring the ice.

Black Ice
after Patrick Rosal

Ice, by nature isn't bad, unless
her Pontiac luges into an oak—furies
in a tailspin
        landing on four lungs
                crushing four limbs.
Her name was Past Closing
which is to say you barely knew her
and to know, I must become
a player in gaslit summer dreams,
follow lightning bug twinkle,
wielding her future
in a box marked
"Address Unknown."

If I mark upon it in a script
comprehensible, it becomes one
of two exact places in time
where so much says so very little.

What I mean is, because the letters
form three lines—tequila / laughter/
a lover / shouldn't mean a life
had to flash
into the sea.

What if I tell you
the wannabe pimp
in line at taco bell
said her ass was fine,
would you answer
with the blood trickle
dividing her forehead?

It's even simpler than that:
you lament the song of Onegin,
banal ballet once on the stage—
the absence of footsteps
holds you alive, Pobrecito.

I'm sorry
the one you once trembled beside
under light falling rivers
(While dancing noiselessly across
a catacomb city lake frozen)
is dead.

Invasive Species

On peninsular Florida
Beware of sand spurs,
Cenchrus echinatus,
Latin for millet
Armed with spines,
Aka
Innocuous grass creeping across the sand.

Cross the gulf, past the tejanos,
Sole suffering's much less nuanced—
Pinche chupacabras, tribulus terrestris,
Perhaps Old-World stowaways
Fastened to rawhide sandals
On the feet of Cabeza de Vaca,
The Moor Estevanico,
And two Spaniards,
A quartet abandoned
In 1527, who spent
An octet of years
Rafting, walking
And butchering their way
From Florida to the Pueblos,
Land of the enchanted,
Now New Mexico true.

Swamp to desert
Slave to healer
Conquistador to horse eater
Finding neither fountains
Of youth or seven cities of Cibola
Only bastions of micaceous mud
And straw, infinite silicate tales,
Brutally economic pantheons
Genetically predisposed to piercing bare souls.

The perennial thorns thrived,
One could even say, proliferated,
Spiking trails, viral mass extinction,
Settler green tentacles
Swallowed the sun,
Casting wide rapacious seeds
Ultimately flowering their own
Little boy mass destruction.

thunderlikeaheart@findme.com

click-bait relationships aside,
i'm mostly into corner store
shelves of unhinged feelings and canned TLC,
the sheer naked necessities,
as it were; i'm a pressurized smoothie
of missed birthdays and lit roman candles,
a parachuting empath

SEEKING

Zodiac Metronome

FOR

long hugs and sexy conversation
on hot wet sand—
god cleared my sinuses
for a reason, you know,
like an army of drooping bats
can only see itself in hindsight—
moonlight's where i'm waiting,
where the largest desert on the planet
makes landfall…

xoxo
#heartsmileemoticon

We Are Each Other's Harvest
after Pablo Neruda

You question me, why is Spider tickling silk
with pine needle toes?
Sand holds the answer, I respond.
You beg of me, what are the hoodoos searching for from castles of
obsidian tears?
What are they looking for? I can only say
They thirst for you, just as I do.
You ask me, who does Coyote serenade,
whose skeletons are scattered in smoke light?
       Watch, listen, wait, let four seasons   gust   and   drift.
You demand answers about wolves running free unaccounted,
      and I reply by detailing
How an elk with an arrow in its hip
      slowly bleeds.
You inquire about the roadrunner's tail,
      fanning salt desert flats?
Or you smell star prints in the selenite rose,
      in the rabid construction
Of the needy and lonely cholla—you'll read my horoscope now?
You wish to comprehend midnight lightning glyphs?
The ghost-eating puma who screams?
The buzz of rattle coiled tight, unwinding
Like the wisp of a river's descent?
I want to tell you that Desert, these hides cling to her flesh, that each
      grain of sand
is an infinite sea, impossible to clothe, muted,
and moths carry mystic hummingbird prayers
seeding secrets
      in arroyo
      yuccas of gold.
I am naught but bats shattering night, sprung from the bowels
      of empty, invisible,
swinging off nebulous slivers, twirling unending void.
I wandered far as you do, interrogating
      moon rocks for clues
And in my blankets, I woke up naked,
My only companion: scorpions chanting wind home.

Most Dangerous Man Alive

He was the most dangerous
man alive, according to Dad,
who three years earlier
put a gun to his own gut only
to rise from the dead unrepentant
and undiagnosed. No choice
but to believe him, for sure, the
turquoise exterior white leather interior
Ford Galaxie 500, 1965 with a 390,
Johnny Cash blasting from dash
board speakers, unfiltered smoke rolled
sleeve white T, black hair siphoned
into a freshly paroled wave
only cool in the South by then
made an impression. My cousin's real
Dad lived flash fiction, profiled
in smoke on an east Kentucky hill,
midday reflection off polished Detroit
chrome. What I saw, maybe real,
maybe another myth from the wounded
bear tragedy I lived, shadow of paw
about to fall typecast our lives; every
minute, every movement, every breath held
unscripted repercussions.

That afternoon,
I caught a glimpse
of the sun outside
our blackhole system.

Southpaw

Reciting days of the week,
I repeatedly skipped Wednesday.

Naming crayon colors,
yellow was yaler.

For kindergarten show and tell
I took a blue and red painted coconut

carved into the likeness of Anthony Quinn
playing the role of fictitious Native

American activist Flapping Eagle,
decorated with feathers plucked from

the musty tail of a marble-eyed
taxidermy pheasant my dad's clandestine

and alcoholic girlfriend with the big
aquarium gifted me, then re-enacted for the

horrified class how my brother Teddy and
I hacked the seemingly Mediterranean but

actually, Irish Mexican features of the actor
from a humble coconut
           husk with a machete.

The next day, my mother called the school
to apologize, you see, Teddy was a dog,

it was 1964,

and *Flap, the Last Warrior* would not appear in theaters until 1970.

Maroon Paisley

Granny C stayed with Tip
 and Lucille
     after Green Berry
         returned to the soil.
     "Memaw," we'd holler,
 "What in tarnation?"
     she'd say back,
         or "Lawdy be,"
             pleading for the lord.
                 I figured tar nation
                     to be home entrapment,
             yet Granny C blossomed
         trillium and rhubarb
on a Singer treadle,
     roots buried deep
         beneath yonder hills.

                 In later years,
         her letters brimmed
             curly q's and bible quotes
                 uncontained by punctuation,
                     unregulated threads
                         spinning out a one bulb kitchen,
                         arthritic nobs
                         knuckled blue
         round worn-out fivers
neatly pressed—
     one each
         for my cousins and me—
                         every birthday
                         Christmas
                         and Easter.

14

Buffalo Gourd

Mom doesn't drive at night,
    and I live in the back, a hand
carved paperweight chaperoning
    dead moth dashboard memories
of a 1963 Ford Falcon, blue, the
    hue of petrichor after river valley
storms. Crystals may be found
    decoding shattered bottle floors
of local canyons. Alone beneath
    rhyolite uplifts, under shadows
of lichen framed petroglyphs, I
    approximate the dance of cranes
in ashen bosque mud. Once attracting a mate,
    we no longer conjugate—deep within
earth, ourselves, echo chamber
    mind flies, spirit painted chilicotes
in slow percolation, condensed sunlight
    geometry passing through monsoon clouds
hung in a mica window, your fingers slip away
    to the heart smashing glass on the moonstruck
blossoms of the vines.

Beatles Love Post It

I'd like to be
Under a homonym synonymous
sinuous, sensual belonging free exchange
       Of linguistic gesture, a rifling
       Of pages, diphthongs pinched
Between two flesh worlds
Squid ink chef's plate
Drizzled over couscous,
Fresh pink prawns, curried
Sirens and mermaid tails
       On shore jaguar isle
       On dugout bowl
Crafting synapsis networks
Under the sea, I'd like to be.

Colorado Alligator Farm Fire

Six hundred fifty-one UFOs
        in the sky tonight,
and I'm not right
        in the head,
summer weeds riot early this year
climate change fentanyl body count
on the scoreboard U-Haul out front
bleeding freon and lighter fluid
        on a third-eye teardrop tat
        on the neck of a slow burning fuse
{a blue fire mouse tail
disappears around a corner}—
[northern light crosses
        paint sand dune nights]

    How far need I run
        spring wind trippin' april
            over rusted barbed wire?
                    Screen door soars across shortgrass prairie,
                an awkward bird of closure
            spreads flaming wings behind me.

Stained Glass Wind Chime: Seven Chanate Songs
an unapologetic ode to end rhyming grackles

A plague
of shimmering iridescence,
indigo
dawn to dusk chatroom
in the treehouse pool hall
'cross the narrow boulevard.

Hangin' and bangin'
like me sea breeze paradox
playas on the corn day
after spring tang summer rites,
fall morning scents on their knees
proposing,
why you stamens clustered into leks?

Hotshot, hotspot,
predation protection hypothesis:
crawled
in the woodpile to die
next to a humming
bird bush =
victims unscheduled.

Screech CAR-ta-GEN-aaa in the springtime
yeartime, seventy-three mother
tear time,
picking yards and pickin' cars,
lean beaks chiseled
for obsidian war games.

Seek and destroy
pollinator offspring
hidden in my mainspring
livin in the streetlight killzone.

Time zones, license plates, loony toon PAs
sharkskin jackals wearing ratty feather boas
checkin' IDs
pizza by the slice
sympathetic
pour logic, pure magic, loose traffic
twenty-five pages about love—
makeover time.

17 long tailed grackles in a
pumpkin spice icehouse
out back alley where
the chickens lost their heads,
hate crime prime time
cackle and coo, I'm callin' you
in a soft smack dial tone
no offense my song
in the night air we share.

Perihelion Twilight

Not quite in the uncanny valley
there's a feeling toward melancholy
between sunset and dusk
   an uneasy wading into
   an itchy realization that the ebb
   and flow of tears is inevitable
   as blood coursing capillaries will one
day still, yet sun will continue its nuclear
fusion, and moon will bashfully reveal
and conceal, and where you will be in that
   there and now
is yet to be determined, as sure as
   vanilla orchids bloom
between dismal swamp branches
between hot mosquito bites.

Mile Marker 25

Too windy to sweat
A ruggedly beautiful day
defiant murmurations whipping
forth and back over wind turbine fields
giants, ever-needy cyclops amid parallel
avian migrations and dinosaur trackway two-steps
beneath, a mother and child's footprints alongside, a six hundred
meter high tree uprooted by the wind, hitherto unnoticed by the
    populace
of a small town nearby, obliterating the house unwittingly lingering in
    its shadow.

Born in 1959 in Pewee Valley, Kentucky and raised in southern Ohio, **Doug Bootes** joined the Army straight out of high school. After that, he worked various restaurant jobs, painted in his free time, a childhood interest encouraged by his mother, and hitchhiked around the south. By the time their first daughter Felicia arrived, he and his wife lived on the inland waterway of Treasure Island Florida, where they both worked at a dockside restaurant and he sold his paintings.

Moving to Santa Fe, New Mexico in 1998, he began showing and selling his paintings in galleries there while working various non-restaurant jobs to pay the bills and support the arrival of another daughter Sophia. In 2001, he also began working at the legendary Shidoni bronze foundry and gallery located in Tesuque, New Mexico, adding sculptures articulated in bronze, wood, and stone to his portfolio.

In 2011, Bootes began working towards a degree in business administration at Sante Fe Community College. After failing Accounting II twice, he spontaneously took a fiction writing class and soon after, switched majors to Creative Writing. Finding supporting mentors and winning numerous awards both at the school and with local publications while finishing his AA, he graduated and then enrolled at the nearby Institute of American Indian Arts.

Having shown with several artists over the years who attended the well known arts school, he was aware of the level of professionalism they were able to take their work to, but was unfamiliar with writing programs of any kind, much less one offering an indigenous perspective. It was an epiphany; that experience was life changing. Working as a writing tutor and earning a BFA in Creative Writing in 2017, then an MFA in Poetry two years later, Bootes was invited to teach at the school as an adjunct upon graduation.

2024 sees a transition to spending more time traveling, visiting family, writing of course, and to take over a Santa Fe based native art appraisal business with a focus on repatriating sacred and culturally significant items to their original homes. A deep love of the land wherever he is and the experiences and stories accumulated over decades of countless jobs, locales, and ongoing endeavors continue to inform his poems, fiction and nonfiction.

Milton Keynes UK
Ingram Content Group UK Ltd.
UKHW012002020524
442050UK00004B/226